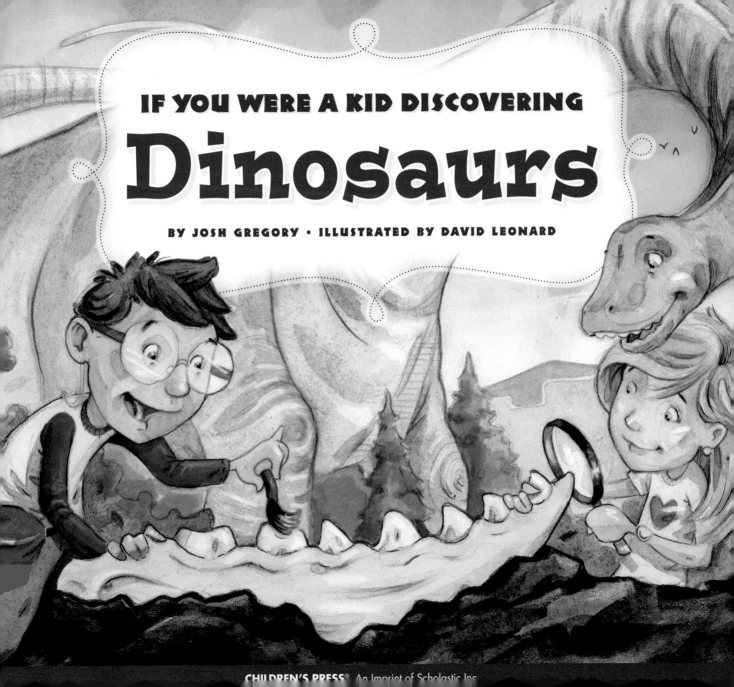

IF YOU WERE A KID DISCOVERING
Dinosaurs

BY JOSH GREGORY • ILLUSTRATED BY DAVID LEONARD

CHILDREN'S PRESS® An Imprint of Scholastic Inc.

Content Consultant
Gregory M. Erickson, PhD, Paleontologist, Department of Biological Science, Florida State University, Tallahassee, Florida

NOTE TO THE READER, PARENT, LIBRARIAN, AND TEACHER: This book combines a historical fiction narrative with nonfiction fact boxes. While all the nonfiction fact boxes are historically accurate and true, the fiction comes solely from the imaginations of the author and illustrator.

Photos ©: 9: Smith Collection/Gado/Getty Images; 11: imageBROKER/Alamy Images; 13: Feature China/Barcroft Images/Barcroft Media/Getty Images; 15: Xavier ROSSI/Gamma-Rapho/Getty Images; 17: dgero/iStockphoto; 19: ZUMA Press/Alamy Images; 21: Corbis/VCG/Getty Images; 23: AlenaPaulus/iStockphoto; 25 left: bendenhartog/iStockphoto; 25 right: Encyclopaedia Britannica/UIG/Getty Images; 27: Richard T. Nowitz/age fotostock.

Library of Congress Cataloging-in-Publication Data
Names: Gregory, Josh, author. | Leonard, David, 1979– illustrator.
Title: If you were a kid discovering dinosaurs / by Josh Gregory ; illustrated by David Leonard.
Other titles: Discovering dinosaurs | If you were a kid.
Description: New York, NY : Children's Press, an imprint of Scholastic Inc., [2017] |
Series: If you were a kid | Includes bibliographical references and index.
Identifiers: LCCN 2017007537| ISBN 9780531237472 (library binding : alk. paper) | ISBN 9780531239483 (pbk. : alk. paper)
Subjects: LCSH: Dinosaurs—Juvenile literature. | Paleontology—Juvenile literature.
Classification: LCC QE861.5 .G757 2017 | DDC 567.9—dc23
LC record available at https://lccn.loc.gov/2017007537

TABLE OF CONTENTS

Looking Into the Past

Long ago, enormous reptiles called dinosaurs roamed our planet. These animals first appeared about 240 million years ago. Over the following 175 million years, many different **species** existed. Some, such as *Tyrannosaurus rex*, were huge. Others, such as *Compsognathus*, were as small as chickens. Some had features such as long necks, deadly horns, or spiked tails.

Dinosaurs died out long before humans existed. However, scientists are able to learn about them by digging up **fossils**. Studying them can tell us where and when prehistoric animals lived, what they looked like, and what they ate.

Turn the page to go on an incredible fossil-finding adventure. You will see that discovering a dinosaur can be a thrilling glimpse into the past.

Meet Miguel!

Miguel Martin loves dinosaurs more than anything. He spends all his free time reading about them, watching movies about them, and drawing pictures of them. He also keeps a close eye on all the latest news about dinosaur discoveries. Miguel's greatest dream is to become a scientist and one day make important discoveries of his own . . .

Meet Ruth!

Ruth Page is Miguel's best friend. She thinks he spends too much time with his nose stuck in dinosaur books. Ruth would much rather play and explore outside. Her favorite thing to do is go on long hikes through forests, mountains, and other natural areas. She especially loves taking pictures of the amazing things she sees on her hikes . . .

Miguel couldn't believe what he was reading. A totally new dinosaur had been discovered. It was one of the biggest ones ever found. He jumped up and ran to ask his dad if they could go see it.

"It's very interesting, but that museum is too far away," Miguel's dad answered.

"Please, Dad," said Miguel. "I'd do anything to see it!"

"I'm sorry," his dad replied. "We just can't afford a trip like that right now."

STUDYING THE PAST

The study of dinosaurs and other ancient life-forms is called **paleontology**. Paleontologists use their knowledge of **geology** and **biology** to study fossils. Only some of them focus on dinosaurs. Others study ancient plants, sea creatures, insects, and other living things.

This fossil of an ancient fish was discovered in Wyoming.

The next day, Miguel was hanging out with Ruth in her tree house. He told her all about the new dinosaur news and how he wanted to see the exhibit.

"Museums are boring anyway," said Ruth. "Even some big new dinosaur can't make them fun."

"I think they're great!" Miguel replied.

"I know," said Ruth. "I'm just teasing. Why don't you come with my family on our hike tomorrow? It will help you forget all about fossils."

HOW ARE FOSSILS FORMED?

There are several main kinds of fossils. Stony fossils form when bones or other pieces of animals are **petrified** over time. Mold fossils form when part of an animal's shape, such as a footprint, is pressed into mud that hardens over time. Cast fossils form when a mold fossil gets filled with mud. This mud dries into the shape of the object that made the mold fossil. Finally, pieces of animals are sometimes preserved in ice or **amber**.

This *Parasaurolophus* skeleton was petrified and preserved as a fossil.

Ruth was right. Miguel was having a great time on the hike. The two friends were amazed by the rock formations they saw as they walked along the sandy path. They pointed out their favorite ones and stopped often to take pictures. But then, Ruth spotted something that seemed out of place.

"What is that sticking out of the ground?" she asked.

Everyone headed toward the strange object.

"Oh wow," Miguel said. "It looks like a dinosaur bone!"

NEW DISCOVERIES

Fossils have taught us a lot about dinosaurs. Also, new discoveries sometimes show older ideas about dinosaurs to be untrue. For example, people long thought that most dinosaurs had lizard-like skin. However, recent discoveries show that many dinosaurs were covered in feathers. Paleontologists still have a lot to learn about these ancient animals.

Look at this piece of a dinosaur tail fossilized in amber. It is covered in feathers!

"That's crazy," said Ruth. "It can't really be a dinosaur bone."

But when everyone gathered for a close look, they had to agree with Miguel. It was a huge bone.

"What should we do?" asked Ruth's dad. "Is there someone we should tell about this?"

"Call the museum," Miguel replied. "They can send paleontologists to dig it up!"

FOSSIL DISCOVERY

Fossils are often discovered sticking out of the ground when weather wears away the soil. Others are found when people dig underground for construction projects. When this happens, paleontologists might search the rest of the area for more fossils. Other times, they look for places where certain types of rocks are common. This is because fossils often tend to be preserved inside these kinds of rocks.

This fossilized leg bone of a *Jobaria* was found in Niger.

Over the next few days, Miguel and Ruth couldn't stop thinking about the discovery. Was it a dinosaur fossil? One afternoon, when they were hanging out at Ruth's house, they got a phone call from the museum. It was good news. They really had found a dinosaur bone! Even better, a team of paleontologists had found more fossils nearby. They invited the kids to visit the dig site.

THE MOST MODERN RELATIVES

Dinosaurs died out millions of years ago. However, many of their relatives are still alive. Studying fossils has taught scientists that dinosaurs are the **ancestors** of today's bird species. Birds have a lot in common with dinosaurs. They breathe the same way. They lay eggs and raise their young the same way. Dinosaurs probably moved and acted a lot like birds, too.

Fossils show that dinosaurs laid eggs much like birds.

At the dig site, the scientists gave Miguel and Ruth a tour. They showed off all the fossils they had found so far. They also demonstrated their digging techniques and equipment. Miguel was amazed by everything he saw. It was a dream come true for him. Even Ruth got caught up in the excitement.

"I didn't realize how much exploring and digging paleontologists did," she said.

"Of course!" said one of the scientists. "That's half of the fun!"

DIGGING DEEP

Paleontologists use tools such as shovels and drills to dig and break rocks apart. They also take lots of photos and write down notes about the things they see. They must work very carefully to avoid damaging fossils. When they find a fossil, they cut out a big chunk of rock all around it. They might then cover the chunk in a layer of protective **plaster**. The chunk is carefully packed up and sent to a lab to be studied.

Paleontologists apply plaster to a large fossil.

The paleontologist told Ruth and Miguel that this was an especially exciting discovery. "We aren't sure yet, but we think this might be a new species."

Miguel couldn't believe what he was hearing. "This is amazing!" he yelled to Ruth. "And we were here to see it happen!"

"Without your help, we wouldn't have known it was here," the paleontologist added.

CLEANING A FOSSIL

Once paleontologists are back in their lab, they work to remove the extra rock from around a fossil. This is a slow, careful process. Scientists use everything from needles and brushes to electric grinders to clear away the dirt and rock. As they work, they continue to take pictures and record their observations. They may also need to figure out how broken fossil pieces fit together.

This fossilized jawbone belonged to a duck-billed dinosaur.

A few weeks later, Miguel and Ruth were back in the tree house. The excitement had died down, and the scientists had gone back to their lab.

"What do you think will happen with our dinosaur?" Ruth asked.

"They'll put it up for people to see at the museum," Miguel answered. "Right next to the other new species I wanted to see."

He sighed. He still wished he could visit the museum and see its fossil collection.

MILLIONS OF YEARS AGO

Paleontologists have two main ways of figuring out how old a fossil is. One is to study how deep underground a fossil is compared to other nearby fossils and rocks. The other is to perform chemical tests on the fossils and rocks in a lab. Knowing a fossil's age helps paleontologists figure out when certain species first appeared, when they became **extinct**, and other important information.

The rock layers surrounding a fossil can help determine its age.

Miguel's wish came true. The museum decided to host a ceremony revealing the new fossils. As the dinosaur's discoverers, Miguel and Ruth were the guests of honor. They got to stand right next to the paleontologists. When the time came, they pulled the curtain to reveal the fossilized skeleton behind it. The audience clapped and cheered.

HOW DID DINOSAURS DISAPPEAR?

By about 66 million years ago, most dinosaur species were extinct. Scientists are not sure exactly why these animals died out. New diseases or changes in weather might have played a role. Most experts believe that an asteroid crashed into Earth, causing all the dinosaurs to die. Whatever the cause, no dinosaur species survived except for their bird **descendants**.

Modern bird

Dinosaur

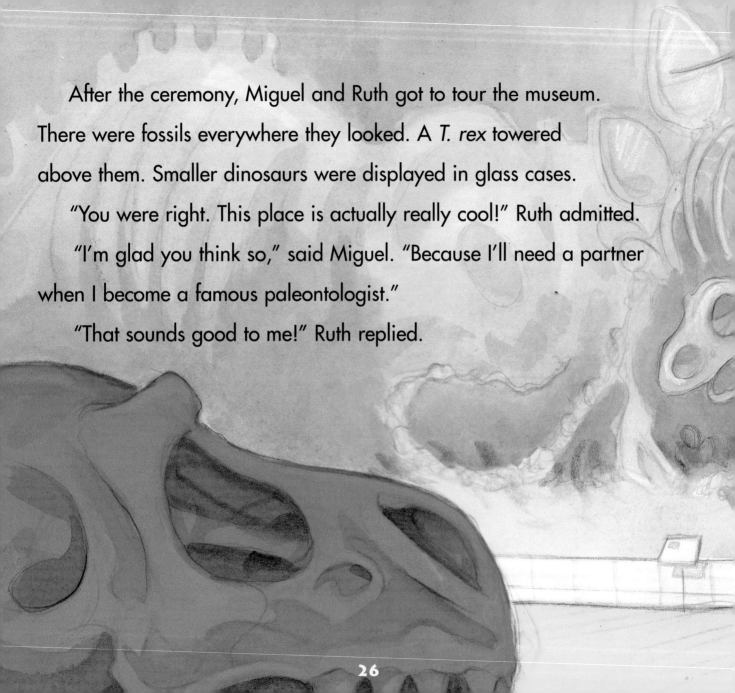

After the ceremony, Miguel and Ruth got to tour the museum. There were fossils everywhere they looked. A *T. rex* towered above them. Smaller dinosaurs were displayed in glass cases.

"You were right. This place is actually really cool!" Ruth admitted.

"I'm glad you think so," said Miguel. "Because I'll need a partner when I become a famous paleontologist."

"That sounds good to me!" Ruth replied.

NOT THE REAL THING

The dinosaur fossils you see in a museum are not always real. Real fossils can be **fragile**. Often, they are missing pieces. Museums may create fake fossils for display. First, they make a mold of the real fossil. Then they fill the mold with plaster or other materials. When the filling dries, it gets hard and looks like a real fossil. Paleontologists also use plaster to sculpt missing pieces of bones and other fossils.

A dinosaur skeleton

Dinosaur Discoveries in the United States

Faith, South Dakota
"Sue," the largest and most complete
T. rex skeleton ever discovered,
is found in 1990.

Denver, Colorado
The first *Triceratops* fossil is
discovered in 1887.

Rocky Mountains
Paleontologists Othniel Marsh and
Edward Cope discover 136 new dinosaur
species during the late 1800s.

Ghost Ranch, New Mexico
Hundreds of complete
Coelophysis skeletons are
discovered together in 1947.

New Jersey
The first partially complete
dinosaur skeleton discovered
in America is found in 1858.

Timeline

1676   A leg bone of a *Megalosaurus* is discovered in England. At the time, scientists think it belongs to a giant human.

1842   Paleontologist Richard Owen coins the term *dinosaur*, meaning "terrible lizard."

1922   Dinosaur eggs are discovered in the Gobi Desert.

2014   Paleontologists unearth a new species of *Titanosaur* in Patagonia, Argentina. It is the largest dinosaur discovered to date.

2016   In Myanmar, a piece of a dinosaur's tail—complete with feathers, skin, and muscle—is discovered preserved in amber.

Words to Know

amber (AM-bur) a yellowish-brown substance formed from fossilized tree sap

ancestors (AN-ses-turz) related species that lived long ago

biology (bye-AH-luh-jee) the study of life and all living things

descendants (di-SEN-duhnts) new species that are related to older ones

extinct (ik-STINGKT) no longer found alive

fossils (FAH-suhlz) any preserved trace of ancient life

fragile (FRAJ-uhl) easily broken

geology (jee-AH-luh-jee) the study of Earth's layers of soil and rock and how they change over time

paleontology (pay-lee-uhn-TAH-luh-jee) the study of ancient life

petrified (PET-ruh-fide) changed into stone

plaster (PLAS-tur) a soft mixture of lime, sand, and water that forms a smooth, hard surface as it dries

species (SPEE-sheez) one of the groups into which plants and animals are divided

Index

ABOUT THE AUTHOR

Josh Gregory is the author of more than 90 books for kids. He has written about everything from animals to technology to history. A graduate of the University of Missouri–Columbia, he currently lives in Portland, Oregon.

ABOUT THE ILLUSTRATOR

David Leonard began his freelance illustration career in the first grade, trading colorings for pencils. Since then, he has worked with clients such as Amazon, Major League Baseball, Dr. Pepper, Warner Music, *Highlights for Children* and *The New Yorker*. When David is not illustrating, he enjoys feeding his snails and flying with his loving, forgiving, understanding, supportive wife and their little, art-directing twin daughters.

Visit this Scholastic website for more information about dinosaurs:

www.factsfornow.scholastic.com

Enter the keyword **Dinosaur**